Anniversary of the Air

Books by Michael Waters:

Anniversary of the Air (1985)
Dissolve to Island: On the Poetry of John Logan (1984)
Not Just Any Death (1979)
Fish Light (1975)

Anniversary

of the

Air

Michael Waters

Carnegie-Mellon University Press
Pittsburgh

ACKNOWLEDGMENTS

The Antioch Review: "Dogs in the Storm"; *Bluefish:* "After Desire"; *Crazyhorse:* "The Stories in the Light," "Bonwit Teller" & "Hair"; *Footprint Magazine:* "The Bicycle"; *The Georgia Review:* "The Faithful" & "Anniversary of the Air"; *Ironwood:* "Punch-Drunk"; *Memphis State Review:* "Carousel"; *The Missouri Review:* "American Bandstand," "Monopoly" & "Green Shoes"; *The Ohio Review:* "Singles" & "Lunch Hour"; *Ploughshares:* "Mythology"; *Poetry:* "The Mystery of the Caves" & "Pollen"; *Three Rivers Poetry Journal:* "Negative Space" & "A Romance"; *The Yale Review:* "The Story of the Caul"

Several poems were reprinted in PUSHCART PRIZE IX: BEST OF THE SMALL PRESSES (Pushcart, 1984), ANTHOLOGY OF MAGAZINE VERSE & YEARBOOK OF AMERICAN POETRY (Monitor, 1984), THE GENERATION OF 2000: CONTEMPORARY AMERICAN POETS, edited by William Heyen (Ontario Review Press, 1984), NEW AMERICAN POETS OF THE 80's, edited by Jack Myers & Roger Weingarten (Wampeter, 1984) & THE MORROW ANTHOLOGY OF YOUNGER AMERICAN POETS, edited by David Bottoms & Dave Smith (Morrow, 1985).

"Dogs in the Storm" appeared as a limited-edition pamphlet (Breakwater Press, 1981). Special thanks to Howard & Laurie Aaron.

Several poems were included in the pamphlets AIR TOUCHED BY THE AXE (Porch, 1980), THE STORIES IN THE LIGHT (Thunder City, 1983) & THE FAITHFUL (raccoon, 1984).

I want to thank the Corporation of Yaddo for residencies, the Salisbury State College Foundation, Inc. for a research grant, & the Maryland State Arts Council for a Literary Work-in-Progress Grant.

The publication of this book is supported by grants from the National Endowment for the Arts in Washington, D.C., a Federal agency, and from the Pennsylvania Council on the Arts.

811.54
W31a
145909
Feb. 1989

CONTENTS

I.

II.

III.

for Robin

In the morning there was a big wind blowing and the waves were running high up on the beach and he was awake a long time before he remembered that his heart was broken.

—Ernest Hemingway
"Ten Indians"

I

THE MYSTERY OF THE CAVES

I don't remember the name of the story,
but the hero, a boy, was lost,
wandering a labyrinth of caverns
filling stratum by stratum with water.

I was wondering what might happen:
would he float upward toward light?
Or would he somersault forever
in an underground black river?

I couldn't stop reading the book
because I had to know the answer,
because my mother was leaving again—
the lid of the trunk thrown open,

blouses torn from their hangers,
the crazy shouting among rooms.
The boy found it impossible to see
which passage led to safety.

One yellow finger of flame
wavered on his last match.
There was a blur of perfume—
mother breaking miniature bottles,

then my father gripping her,
but too tightly, by both arms.
The boy wasn't able to breathe.
I think he wanted me to help,

but I was small, and it was late.
And my mother was sobbing now,
no longer cursing her life,
repeating my father's name

among bright islands of skirts
circling the rim of the bed.
I can't recall the whole story,
what happened at the end . . .

Sometimes I worry that the boy
is still searching below the earth
for a thin pencil of light,
that I can almost hear him

through great volumes of water,
through centuries of stone,
crying my name among blind fish,
wanting so much to come home.

AMERICAN BANDSTAND

The boy rehearsing the Continental Stroll
before the mirror in his bedroom —
does he memorize the sweep of hair
tumbling across his eyes
when he spins once, then claps his hands?

Home from school in winter,
he studies the couples on television,
their melancholy largo,
how they glide together, then separate.
Such dancing makes him nervous —
so many hand motions to remember,
where to slide his feet, and
every girl in the gym staring at him.

That boy was familiar, twenty years ago,
saying hello to a loneliness
peculiar to the tender, the high-strung
lanterns suspended above the dance floor,
ousting shadows, leaving him
more alone, trapped in the spotlight.

The Peppermint Twist, The Bristol Stomp,
The Hully Gully are only memory,
but loneliness still dances
among the anxious ghosts of the heart,
preparing to stroll
down a line formed by teenagers
mouthing lyrics, clapping hands,
forever awkward,
each partner dreaming of grace.

MYTHOLOGY

Because no one has ever asked,
because the task is incumbent upon me,
I want to reveal the secret
gathering place of heroes:

we scaled the rough, stucco wall
of a row of one-story garages
and loitered on the tar roof,
staring down the weakening sun —

Tommy O'Brien, Glenn Marshall,
everyone's girl, Rosemarie Angelastro,
and the dumb kid, Gregory Galunas,
who let ants walk on his tongue.

We smoked butts and told no one.
Once Billy McAssey jumped
and stove the canvas top
of a cream-and-blue convertible.

At five o'clock the mothers
groaned their chorus from the curb,
each name shouted like a warning
to the worn men leaving work.

But I remained on the roof
till lights blinked on in tenements,
the smell of fish oiled the air,
and radios sent forth tinny polkas . . .

and through a tinted wing of glass
began to read the heavens,
the bright syllables of stars,
as words took shape, lyrical prose,

a whole story
filled with heroes, their great names,
their impending deaths praised
on the darkening pages of the sky.

A smart kid,
when I asked my spiritless father,
"Where do the dead go?"
I already knew the answer.

THE BICYCLE

I don't want anyone to explain
this bicycle brought across the ocean.
The streets of the new world
are paved, if lucky,

by husbands who surrender trade
to the steam of tar, who
labor with such precise sorrow
their sons soon leave home.

Photographs become precious:
how proud she looks beside her bicycle!
And in her eyes, here,
that particular shade of green

must still burn
to bargain marriage, cross
borders toward the year of my birth.
One family

breeds the immigration
officials, the next
reasons for fleeing continents —
I don't want anyone to explain.

Any way you try to make sense
of the past . . . sighs my father,
shuffling photographs,
revising the pale histories . . .

but this bicycle blazes in sunlight!

FIRST LOVE

So what if you're living in Jersey
with a man who works for the phone company.
Your life must be miserable—
a name lost in a row of mailboxes

studding the loud, gravel drive,
your husband shaking the whole trailer
when he grunts onto you each night,
his workshirts souring in one corner.

So what if none of this is true
and your daughters grow lovely on lawns,
if your husband steps off the 5:14
asking, "Can we do nothing this evening?"

I imagine the fireplace, the flokati rug,
the cat sighing on her silk pillow.
So what if I live just across the river
and speak to the immigrant shopkeepers

or to no one, so what if I chain
my dog to a hydrant for hours, so what
if I buy a single pork chop for dinner.
So what if this life flows on, if I read

a passage in some Russian novella
and think of you, if I go to the table
to write this poem, but have nothing to say
except *so what, so what, so what?*

SINGLES

I don't know anyone more lonely
than the woman listening
to the late news, memorizing
baseball scores for coffee break.

She must undress so carefully,
folding her beige blouse
as if for the last time,
not wanting to be found unkempt

by detectives in the morning.
Sometimes I hear her talking
as she roams from room to room
watering her plumeria,

the only splash of color.
She sets two places at the table
though no one ever comes,
then turns to the boredom of bed

thinking *Indians 7 - Yankees 3,
Cardinals 11 - Mets 2*
until she rises before dawn
and drives crosstown to work.

Could anyone be more lonely?
She doesn't acknowledge, again,
the man in the toll-booth
who's spent the whole night there,

not even a magazine before him,
grateful now to be making change
and touching fingers, briefly,
with such a beautiful stranger.

THE FAITHFUL

Sometimes, when the world
no longer seems capable of surprise,
when your wife rehearses
the usual gestures of affection

and birches offer their annual
assortment of autumn leaves,
you forget how small the heart
might be, how fragile.

One morning, rushing to work,
you brush past a stranger
more beautiful than the dark
bruise of adolescence —

your fingers tracing a breast
at fourteen, your tongue
blooming with the moisture
on your sweetheart's throat —

and the world fashions a frail
shell, a pale rind,
the air within billowing
with the scent of buds unfolding,

so that in the story
you'll tell tonight to your children,
the cobbler in a barren country
lets fall his apron

to find, not nails, but
breathing, miraculous roses.

MONOPOLY

The loneliness of two people
together, rolling dice
as if their luck might change,
arrives with the breeze

of moths fanning a lampshade,
casual, without voice—
so the radio keeps reciting
those brokenhearted syllables

that tumble through the open
window onto the wet street.
When I glance up, I can see
the woman dancing, alone,

while her husband swaps deeds,
steers a miniature, silver
racer along the boardwalk
or, worse, drags a worn shoe

onto Baltic Avenue, past peep-shows
where couples simulate sex
on screens flecked with grime.
This game seems crazy to her

because it holds the boredom
back only a few minutes, because
no one can possess the night.
Her husband thinks she's silly,

so the board is folded,
the money stacked by color,
and water runs in the bathroom
for a long time. But, in bed,

they pull each other close,
and why not? — each hauling
the other like found junk,
hoping to become something more

valuable, less bankrupt,
before the slow irony of dawn,
before the next cast of moon.
Together, in their yellow room,

they level their account:
a little motion that might pass
for travel, an overwhelming
desire to win without luck.

CAROUSEL

Logic tells me the fabulous creatures
carved for this turn-of-the-century
carousel never existed,
though children who ride them
later dream them into breath,
their beds spinning upward
toward the lost, morning stars.

Over the seawall, a bell
tolls across avenues of spray,
echoing in the pavilion
where the griffon feigns sleep.
Twisted brass poles refuse
to glint in the salt,
though last night a girl's
blown hair dusted the cracked,
spiraling horn of the unicorn.

I woke here before the sun broke
open the ocean's blue sheen, rising
upon abandoned ferris-wheels & bumper cars,
the million mirrors empty, their bulbs
yellow & fading. Yet
these fabulous creatures remain, poised
as if transformed by dawn into stone.

I wanted to straddle the rough scales
    of the dragon,
traveling nowhere, posing
for an imaginary photograph to send
to several childhood friends, but
the entrance was barred

and a guard posted by the pier.

Now I remember another year, a carousel
spinning off the blank shore of Brooklyn,
   one human figure
swimming through such rarefied air—
a mermaid streaming long, green hair.
I sat upon her slender waist,
clutching a sleek fin, & closed my eyes
as we parted pale curtains of water.
She was lovely as my young mother
and we needed no one but each other.

II

DOGS IN THE STORM

after Akhmatova

When this slow heart was raging
and I could tell no one, especially you,
I would abandon the exhaustion of sheets,
this woman tossing like damp leaves,

and storm a few miles into the country.
I wanted to memorize the silhouette
of each branch, the chorus of stars,
the uproar of the willows' shadows,

the stiff mailboxes bearing witness
to such immense drift and flux.
I wanted to not think about you.
But each time some stray bitch

came limping along the highway,
eyes iced shut in the wind, nose
scenting the hunger of wild couplings,
I wondered: Whose lost lover is this?

And how far away is my distant brother
who howls for us both in such savage moonlight?

THE STORIES IN THE LIGHT

stopping on the green
   uniform of the schoolgirl
      crossing Fifth Avenue—

her fingers smoothing the skirt
   against gusts, against thighs,
      while holding her hat to her hair—

begin to come true those evenings
   after the skirt has been folded,
      the legs bathed and forgotten:

now your lover inherits a past
   fashioned from such pure moments,
      lovely before you knew her,

before the light began traveling
   and gathered you together,
      because such stories at best

are false, cut-out silhouettes,
   because the past changes
      each time traffic stalls,

because the light one particular
   autumn afternoon struck me
      and I have never seen it again,

but I have this task:
   to consider the source of stories,
      to allow that skinny schoolgirl

to blossom into someone's lover,
   maybe yours, maybe mine,
      though even now she is sleeping.

NEGATIVE SPACE

When you press next to me
on the downtown local, calm
in the clamor of secretaries,
the vast alarum of wheels,

toting your new sketchpad,
I imagine the flexed muscles
of the male model, the art
class you audit each night.

No one else notices you,
not even when the lights fail
and the train halts between stations,
when the air in the car grows stale

and, aloud, you begin to count
express trains flickering toward Queens.
Their lit windows bear faces
schoolchildren draw

in pencil on each fingernail,
though these faces are dimmer,
thinking of supper, thinking of bed,
the four hours of boredom between . . .

The lesson this evening will be
to see what is *not* there,
to draw "negative space,"
the space, say, between two bodies,

say yours and mine, so palpable,
milky as the pulp
of the wet, green pears
ignored on the stool before you.

Their odor inhabits the air
so that, hours later,
entering your apartment,
the key still fixed in the lock,

you stare at the familiar furniture—
the sofa-bed with its worn print,
the table with one leg
propped on newspaper,

the vase with its red, silk flower—
and see, not these still-lifes, but
the terrible, torn spaces between them
you must, this moment, begin to fill.

PUNCH-DRUNK

It's when the brains get shook up
and run together that you get
punch-drunk.   —Sonny Liston

Tough guys swayed with Archie Moore
when his legs began to go,
that heavy surf slowing
the late rounds, each jab

blurring the ropes, the lights
liquid, his body begging
to drift with dignity down.
No easy thing to quit the ring.

When I faced a former lover
in Rockefeller Center, crowds hushed
as if a left hook had connected,
so I blinked through water,

and almost started to swim
Sixth Avenue in delirium,
before slurring some dumb greeting,
then stumbling toward the corner bar.

I can still see that submerged
corridor, and celebrate Archie Moore,
ex-champ, visiting Stillman's gym,
his world frozen for a moment—

the heavy bags, sparring partners,
the hungry shadows punching walls—
until the contenders resume,
having nodded their respect,

and sweat thaws the silence
that had broken open the air.

A ROMANCE

The couple arguing on Tenth Street—
"You've ruined it, Jenny," he shouts,
"you've ruined the Fourth of July!"—
halts my favorite waste of time:

reading titles on dust-jackets
lining the top shelves of bookcases
glimpsed through windows at night.
Jenny looks more than familiar—

once seen with some degree of intimacy.
Does anyone here recognize her?—
not the vendor on his corner
staining scoops of shaved ice—

cherry, lemon, grape—with patriotic
fervor, not the doberman
straining the leash to avoid them.
His voice carries to the upper stories.

Now I remember where I've seen her:
the inside cover of *The New Yorker*
modeling a Bali bra
in the lobby of some swank hotel.

Jenny rushes now through leaf-shadow
toward the clamor of Washington Square,
while the guy spits on the sidewalk,
then fixes me with his stare.

I return to the rows of books
luminous as a fireworks display:
THE AGE OF INNOCENCE, PORTRAIT OF A LADY,
LYRICS by Edna St. Vincent Millay.

AFTER DESIRE

touch revises the obscure passages,
the brief alphabet lovers invent
below bridges, in unswept doorways,
shooting stars like apostrophes,

the red ellipses of taxis
trailing into terminals, into tunnels.
After desire, the body's
no longer a lexicon of moans,

and the wind hewing the billboards
no teenager's wild anthem —
splintered syllables, spray of vowels —
but articulate, composed,

reedy with knowledge like the slender
shock of verbena, so purple,
its fragrance in the air's pitch
flushing the face with a bridal

wreath — her lips on your brow —,
with the promise of a language
exhausted now, but
not lost forever, after desire.

BONWIT TELLER

Who says the light doesn't breathe
or press its thumbprint of snow
upon this rouged cheek
mirrored in the store window?

We stare—
                    this reflection and I—
as she brushes her frosted hair
with her fingers, without regard
for little winds that tease the ends.

Above the roofs, the roof of snow
slowly collapses, but never touches
this landscape, so tropical,
where three mannequins,
                                    almost nude
in the luminous, sand-strewn solitude,
        model bright bikinis—
stars wished above polished knees.

These familiar women also stare
into the fierce and artificial glare
of the yellow, foil sun—
while I pause among them, plump
ghost in a wet, woolen coat,
foolishly brushing my dampening hair.

Couldn't these sisters have prophesied
from their boiling cauldron of sun
what the future stores for flesh?—
how the various lights stress
each withering imperfection?

As a schoolgirl I stopped before this window,
closed my eyes, and rocked upon my flats

until the sidewalk seemed to undulate
and I grew dizzy with despair.
Will the change come? I sighed,
wanting to blossom into the sleek
skins, glossy thighs, impossible waists,
     bracelets and silver fox capes
that pronounced each flake of light.

Even their lashes were lovely, spidering
eyes opened forever in the stunned,
violet gaze of the paralyzed.
Will the change come soon?
Theirs was a perfect, breathless world.
The city could not touch them.

And I? — I stamp my galoshes for warmth,
embarrassed for the woman of snow
embarrassed now among them.
Their world remains, and remains
more eloquent than mine.

I realize the lateness of the hour, realize . . .
the buses will not run on time.

Only the glittering, gypsy taxis
like scarabs along the avenue,
the rows of traffic lights
shuttering — yellow,
           now red, now green —
a universe of diminishing suns,
and the million, heaving snowflakes
    light my skin
as if transforming me
          Will the change come?
into a speechless mannequin.

LUNCH HOUR

for Jody Swilky

In the newspaper, another feature
  on the welder who fell six stories
    and lived, his impression

upon the blue roof of the Oldsmobile,
  his return, weeks later, to the site.
    Who expects such miracles these days?

Eating a ham sandwich, the mustard
  spicy on his tongue, he felt lucky:
    the city spread below him to the river,

the faded denim of sky,
  the sunlight celebrating anniversaries
    upon the rough architecture of his cheek.

Lunch hour, twenty minutes to the whistle,
  and nothing to do but gaze
    upon pigeons floating like paper,

the spires of downtown churches
  announcing their slender faiths.
    Last thing he remembered, he said,

was a shout, probably his own,
  that plunged with him like a bride,
    offering company unto the earth.

There's never a reason for loneliness,
  though it was created
    like this skyscraper, like pigeons

shitting among girders, the glittering cinders,
   eyeing some large, clumsy screech-owl
      who's forgotten how to fly,

but flaps his arms anyway
   on this brief passage
      from one story to the next.

III

THE BLACK SWAN

for Elizabeth Spires

As the black swan bears her grief
and refuses to share it with anyone,
not with the white swans, obedient daughters,
who place their beaks in your palm,
not for a crust of bread, or sunflower seed,

I also refuse to name the sorrow
that floats this poem across the waters,
a schoolboy's paper boat, now in flames,
drawing your attention for a moment
while sailing past, then vanishing,

ghost-among-the-lilies, shimmering negative,
small death given shape
like the lovely, fragile skull of the swan,
the black swan, light flaring from her eyes,
who lends the pond meaning, and depth.

HAIR

I never know how to relax
  once the ambulance whines away,
    hauling another neighbor
      who suffered a massive heart

failure while trimming the hydrangea.
  Under the hedge his shears
    begin to flame in the slow,
      inexorable conspiracy of rust.

I browse through the dust-
  laden volumes along the wall,
    searching for some passage
      that might affirm, give up,

then walk to the barbershop
  to experience the calm
    fingers massaging my scalp,
      the tonics smart in rows

above stacks of *True* and *Cavalier*.
  But the dead man's hair,
    shampooed and cut that morning,
      lies strewn across the floor,

almost hieroglyphic —
  so, after sharing the news,
    I see the barber in the mirror
      stare at the chance designs.

And I remember the stories
  of hair sprouting in coffins,

the man in the iron mask
　　choking on decades of hair,

Medusa's halo of snakes,
　　the yellow hair of Rapunzel
　　　forming a ladder for lovers,
　　　　Hester Prynne's shock

of black, sexual hair
　　undone in a flood of sunshine,
　　　and Whitman's democracy of grass,
　　　　"the beautiful uncut hair of graves,"

until the barber, still hushed,
　　after brushing my neck with talc
　　　and flapping the apron in air,
　　　　bends to grab the dust-

pan and whisk broom,
　　to sweep away the dead
　　　bristles of my beard,
　　　　this bodiless but shining hair.

GREEN SHOES

Those green shoes on the curb
belong to the bum
sleeping in the doorway.
He wants the warmth of the sun

to inhabit them, to last
through another bitter night.
He'll doze until the traffic
grows heavy, businessmen

grinding home, then rise
to slip on those shoes—
still amazed by the perfect
fit, green shoes

thrown away by some big woman
no longer desiring to dance,
whose husband burst his heart
wrestling such strong legs.

He likes to imagine that!—
this bum who bears witness
each day among back alleys,
who tried them on, and grinned,

and tramped off as if owning
the whole blooming world,
still trusting dumb luck,
secure in the knowledge

the lost somehow find shelter,
the crippled always catch up,
the thirsty divine water,
the disinherited are welcomed

home wearing green shoes
polished with spit and sleeve,
green shoes flashing
fortune in the unblinking sunlight.

ORANGES

Athens

At this morning's market the veteran
is selling oranges, blood
oranges spun with a wrist-flick
from crates into rows on the cart.

Last week he peddled lemons, or
offered eggs still flecked with dirt.
Now he splashes water from his pouch
onto the puffed, sweating skins

and bends his leathery neck to bite
the stream. Then again begins
to bark his prices, lower each hour,
the oranges sweetening in the heat,

as his shirt-sleeve comes unpinned
to flap in the air like a flag,
beckoning children to his stall.
He does not fasten the wild uniform.

The ripening fruit has taught him
to let the elements nourish:
the glinting sun, the icy spray,
the breeze hoisting his invisible arm.

Let the seed float, the hatching heart
pump its blood without our will.
Let each creature flourish,
fresh-cut at the navel.

FULTON STREET

How the fish vendor arranges her fish
on the perishing scales of ice,

not by size, or by color,
but by the curve of their fanned tailfins,

this language of red mullet
beckoning her home to the peculiar

light sifting the olive
aisles of water, to the tattered

nets, the shifting skiffs,
the hushed harbor of her dead husband.

ANNIVERSARY OF THE AIR

Past storefronts lit among the dusk-swept avenues
where those broken grandmothers spit
or straighten their babushkas in the smoky light
        of sausages, streaked windows
hung with strings of red and green peppers,
bluefish gazing through galaxies of pink glaze,

she groans up the bursting, rubble-strewn path
where Our Lady of the Ascension
glistens in rain—
to light one candle, by habit, for her husband
who no longer rests, even in memory,
with any detail,

though tonight she might remember his hair,
red as the candle, or
his alert, political mind flickering
like the flame on its black wick.

The seraphic coloratura of the choir
lulls her . . .

She'll hear them later, distinct, bordering
        her bed, cold water
whispering through the walls, whispering
her name—*Anna*—across the vast
privacies of so many years

so that, in sleep, those tongues start to storm
        through her breast and cross the narrows
        of her lips,
cries of homesickness overwhelming the vermilion
        sky of her arrival,

cries of wrenching in bone-weary orgasm mixed
        with the animal cries of her husband,
cries of her daughters awash in the headlights
        of automobiles racing the rose-blown
        wallpaper (or were those her cries too?),
old-language cries across back alleys
        of rug-beatings and boiling laundry,

the last cries transforming into birdsong
        in the crenellated dawn
as she awakens, light-struck, this swallow
        of a woman, to celebrate the past,
        this anniversary of the air
issuing forth
with the now-recalled memory of his hair:

yes, *red*, and for this anniversary—
with thanksgiving to Our Lady—
the color is enough.

POLLEN

You see it as summer begins
    to shimmer on the rims
        of ponds, in rifts
            in stone where ants assume
their awesome responsibilities,
    on eaves of Victorian mansions
        limned with last light —
            pale curtains sweeping
among the generous trees,
    messages sent between green
        families, greetings
            before the heat strikes us
too lazy to speak, or even
    nod in the sullen breeze,
        surging across the vast
            expanses of lawns, past
new screens, tumbling
    through rich stories of air
        to dust floors, mirrors,
            every surface with a frail
film where a boy can trace
    his name, then raise
        the finger to his lips
            to taste the feathery
light, the bright ash, the yellow
    powder etching the whorls
        of his finger's tip with mild
            fire, incandescence,
this swollen glimmer, loose
    spirit, the hours' aura,
        the plush, allusive
            tremble of pollen.

THE STORY OF THE CAUL

When the child woke to the world,
the caul wrapping her breath
like some cheesy cloth, her
eyes filling with the billowing

clouds, the wavering gauze —
little bride, shroud-bearer —
the doctor snipped her pale
veil at the hairline, to

sell to a sailor for luck.
She remembers, she tells me now,
the mist lifting from her face,
the milky web broken,

the opalescent lights blazing back
to her kindling brain,
the shapes swimming before her
assuming flesh, more warmth,

ever more wonder —
and she closed her blue eyes
and slept, and could have been
content not to open them again.

She knows, she tells me now,
how the world begins to come true
if we stare long enough,
if we stare hard.

Be patient, grandmother tells me.
Be still, sometimes,
to allow the numinous net of air
to mend over your face.